DESERTS

ANGELA WILKES

Illustrated by PETER DENNIS

Contents

Consultant: Dr. Andrew Warren
University College London

In the Desert

Deserts are the driest places in the world. In parts of them it may not rain for many years.

Most deserts are very hot in the daytime. But at night they cool down and can be very cold.

WHEN IT RAINS, SAND AND STONES ARE CARRIED DOWN FROM THE HILLS BY FLOODWATER AND LEFT IN FAN-SHAPED PATTERNS ON THE GROUND.

Most deserts are rocky and bare. Parts of them are covered in sand which the wind blows along so that it piles up into dunes.

Few plants and animals can live in the desert because it is too dry. The ones that are there all have ways of living without much water.

THIS PLAIN FLOODS AFTER RAIN. BUT THE RAIN SOON DRIES UP IN THE HOT SUN, LEAVING BEHIND DRY PATCHES OF SALT.

CARAVAN OF CAMELS TAKING SALT ACROSS THE DESERT.

IN PARTS OF DESERTS THERE ARE BIG, STRANGE ROCKS. THEY MAY BE ALL THAT IS LEFT OF A MOUNTAIN.

WHERE THERE IS WATER, IT MAY MAKE AN OASIS— A PLACE WHERE TREES AND PLANTS CAN GROW.

lthough it is hard to find water
nd food in the desert, some people
ve there. Many of them are
omads. They move around from

place to place and set up their
camps wherever they can find a
well or a waterhole.

How the Desert Changes

The wind does strange things in the desert. It whips up spiralling columns of dust.

The wind blows the sand so that it moves and changes direction like ripples on water.

If there is something in the sand's way, such as grass, the sand piles up behind it.

The moving sand usually piles up to make a small hill, called a dune. Sand is blown up one side of a dune, then slides down the other side, which is steeper. This makes the dune move forwards very slowly The sand around dunes is soft and cars can easily get stuck in it.

There was once a river in this desert. It made this channel thousands of years ago.

It washed broken rocks down from the hills. They now lie on the plains below.

Desert rocks slowly change all the time. Wind-blown sand wears them into odd shapes.

Sometimes just part of the rock wears away. This natural rock arch is in Utah, U.S.A.

Many rocks are jagged because sudden rain and heat and cold make bits of them break off.

These spiky rock towers in Bryce Canyon, U.S.A., were once part of an area of high, flat land.

A Storm in the Arizona Desert

BIG TREES HAVE VERY LONG ROOTS TO HELP THEM FIND WATER.

THIS OCTOTILLO BUSH HAS DROPPED ITS LEAVES SO THAT IT DOES NOT NEED SO MUCH WATER.

MANY TREES AND BUSHES GROW NEAR STREAM BEDS, IN WHICH WATER MAY BE STORED.

SANDY STREAM-BED

Everything that grows in the desert needs water. It has not rained here for many months and the ground is hard, dry and dusty.

The plants look dead, but are not. They all have ways of staying alive in the dry season, but they will not grow again until it rains.

6

There are sometimes huge thunderstorms in parts of the desert. Then there is heavy rain. Water races down riverbeds and channels and floods across the plains. Even when the rain stops the water may take weeks to sink into the ground or dry up in the sun.

Spadefoot toad 1

2

3

After the rain, insects hatch and animals come out of their hiding places, like this toad.

It had buried itself to keep moist. Now it comes out to find a mate and lay eggs in the water.

The eggs hatch into tadpoles, which grow into toads before the pools of water dry up.

After the Rain

After the rain green shoots push their way up out of the damp ground, and parts of the desert may be covered in a carpet of flowers.

They have grown from seeds that may have been lying there for many years. The seeds will not grow unless there is plenty of rain.

The flowers only bloom and live for a few weeks, while there is still enough water for them.

Insects come to drink nectar from them and spread pollen from one flower to another.

This helps the flowers to make new seeds, which will flower after the next rain.

Some plants can live in the desert all the year round because they store water.

Barrel cactus

BEFORE RAIN

AFTER RAIN

There are many kinds of cactus in America. They have tough skins but are juicy inside.

When it rains, their widespread roots soak up water and their stems swell to store it.

Cacti have flowers but have spines instead of leaves, to protect them from thirsty animals.

Saguaros

Cissus plant (Africa)

Welwitschia (Africa)

They grow very slowly but some grow very tall. Cacti like this may be over 100 years old.

This shrub also stores water in its stem. Some desert trees store water in their trunks.

This plant collects dew on its leaves. Drops of water then drip to the ground above its roots.

9

Birds that live in the Desert

Desert birds all have special ways of living with the heat and shortage of water.

Flocks of budgerigars live in the Australian Outback. They drink at waterholes.

If it does not rain for a long time and the waterholes dry up, thousands of them die.

The ostrich can go for days without drinking. It breathes fast to help it keep cool.

Birds that eat seeds must drink every day. The sand grouse flies a long way to find water.

It wets its breast feathers and flies back to its chicks, who suck the water from them.

Vultures keep cool by soaring high in the sky. Their sharp eyes can spot a dead animal to eat from many miles away. When they see one they swoop down to feed. They get the liquid they need from their prey's blood. Small birds get liquid by eating juicy insects.

Birds must shield their eggs from the sun. The gila woodpecker builds its nest in a cactus.

When it leaves the hole it has made, another bird, such as this owl, moves in.

The burrowing owl makes its nest in a burrow that a prairie dog once lived in.

Surviving in the Desert

Deserts are so hot in the daytime that most animals would die if they stayed in the sun for long.

Most desert animals, like these American ones, shelter from the sun during the hottest part of the day.

A BOBCAT DOZES IN THE SHADE OF A BUSH OR ROCK, PANTING TO HELP IT KEEP COOL. IT GOES HUNTING AT NIGHT, WHEN THE DESERT IS COOLER.

THE AMERICAN DESERT TORTOISE SOMETIMES BURROWS UNDERGROUND TO HIDE FROM THE SUN.

HORNED LIZARD PARTLY BURIED IN THE SAND.

CORAL SNAKE

Even reptiles, such as snakes and lizards, which have tough leathery skins to protect them, look for shade when it is hot.

Desert animals must be able to live without much water. Most of them get the liquid they need from the plants or insects they eat.

The jack rabbit's huge ears help it to keep cool, as well as to hear enemies coming.

The addax antelope lives in the Sahara. It does not drink any water at all.

Camels can go without water for weeks, but then they drink gallons at a time.

SIDEWINDER RATTLESNAKE

This rattlesnake has buried itself in the sand to keep cool, and to lie in wait for victims.

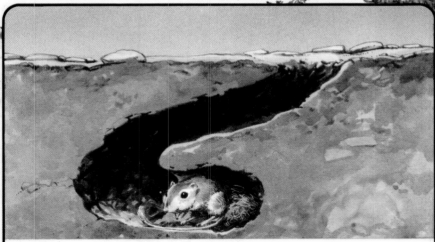

The kangaroo rat digs a shallow burrow where it can hide and sleep during the day.

It does not drink any water. It gets all the moisture it needs from the seeds it eats.

Hunters and the Hunted

Most desert animals hunt at night. The kit fox's sand-coloured fur is good camouflage.

It hunts kangaroo rats. They jump high, kicking sand in the fox's face, then run away.

Some lizards, like this Australian one, have a spiny skin to protect them from enemies.

How a rattlesnake hunts

1

2

The rattlesnake is poisonous, but will not attack large animals unless frightened. It shakes the rattle on its tail as a warning.

But it is quiet at night when it hunts. Small pits near its eyes and its forked tongue help it to sense when a small animal is near.

14

When this Australian lizard is in danger, it puffs out its frill to frighten its attacker.

The scorpion kills insects with the poisonous sting at the end of its tail.

This small trapdoor spider makes traps for insects to fall into, then it eats them.

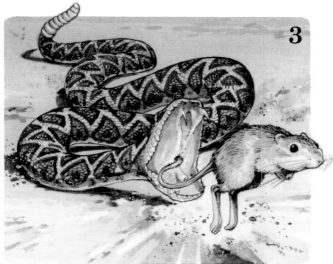

3

The snake glides silently forwards, then it quickly strikes. It sinks its poisonous fangs into its prey and then it lets it go.

4

The animal runs away but dies very quickly. The snake goes after it. When it finds the dead animal, it swallows it whole.

Living in the Desert – 1

Living in the desert is difficult because water and food are hard to find. Many desert people are nomads and move from place to place.

The Tuaregs are nomads who live in the Sahara. They are herdsmen and travel from well to well, looking for pastures for their animals.

The Tuaregs were once fierce warriors who lead great camel raids. They do not fight now.

They wear loose robes, to keep cool. Round their necks they hang charms against evil.

Tuareg men keep their faces veiled. The veil, called a tagilmust, is six metres long.

The Tuaregs keep camels, goats and sheep. They always camp near a well or waterhole, where the animals can drink and graze.

The women or children fetch water for the camp. They carry it in goatskin containers, which they sling under their mules.

BELONGINGS IN TREE, OUT OF REACH OF ANIMALS

ANIMALS

WATER CONTAINER HANGING FROM TRESTLE

Tuaregs live in tents, which they carry with them. The tents are usually made of goatskins stitched together and stretched over poles.

The women collect firewood and cook the food. Here one woman is making bread while the other grinds corn to make a kind of flour.

Living in the Desert – 2

Not all nomads are like the Tuaregs. The Bushmen of the Kalahari Desert do not keep herds, but collect plants to eat and hunt animals.

They wander from place to place, making grass huts to sleep in at night. Their way of life has not changed for thousands of years.

Every day the women look for roots to eat. They can spot plants even in the driest ground, and then dig them up with sharp sticks.

The men go hunting, using spears and poisoned arrows. There are few animals in the Kalahari and the hunters must track them down.

Bushmen know how to find water under the ground. They suck it up through hollow reeds.

Sometimes they store water in buried ostrich shells, so that they can drink it later.

Australian aborigines used to live like the Bushmen, but now most of them live in towns.

Change for the nomads

When there is a long drought, the waterholes dry up and some nomads move to towns.

Many nomads are now learning to read and write, so they can get jobs if they want to.

More and more men who were nomads get jobs on farms or work in mines to earn a living.

A Sahara Salt Caravan

Some goods are still taken across the desert by caravans of camels. This Tuareg is packing salt to take across the Sahara and sell.

Camels are loaded with the heavy bundles. They can travel for several days without any water but they are sometimes bad-tempered.

The camels are tied together so they follow the leader and cannot run away. The men ride them when the sand is too hot to walk on.

Caravans follow their own routes across the desert. The Tuaregs use the sun and stars, as well as familiar landmarks, to guide them.

Camels are hard to ride at first because they sway from side to side and back and forth. Tuaregs steer them with their feet and a rope.

Camels must drink every few days when they are carrying heavy loads. Tuaregs can sometimes find water under the sand between the wells.

The caravan has to stop when there is a sandstorm. The men let the camels loose and shelter from the sand until the storm is over.

The caravan stops at night and the men sit around a fire drinking tea and telling stories. They sleep wrapped in blankets on the ground.

Oases

An oasis is a place in the desert where there is water, either from a spring or from a river, and where trees and plants can grow.

Most oases, like this Tunisian one, have towns built around them. People can live here because there is always a supply of water.

People grow fruit trees and vegetables. Date palms grow easily and are useful for food and wood. This man is cutting dates.

There are two kinds of market in Tunisian oasis towns. This is a food market. The food is piled up on woven mats on the ground.

The souk is a covered market where people sell most things apart from food. Caravans bring goods from across the desert to these markets.

Houses in an oasis are usually made of mud or plaster. Their thick walls, flat roofs and small windows help to keep them cool inside.

Troglodyte homes

Some desert people live in very strange places. The Matmatans of Tunisia build their houses under the ground, where it is cooler.

Cones of Cappadocia

On the edge of the desert in Turkey people build houses in these rocks. They hollow out the insides and put in windows and doors.

Strange Sights in the Desert

Thirsty travellers crossing deserts sometimes see a lake shimmering in front of them. But as they move closer, the water disappears.

It is a mirage – a trick of the light. Hot air above the ground acts like a mirror. It reflects the sky and looks like a sheet of water on the ground.

This is also a mirage. These camels are on dry land but they look as if they are walking in water and we can see their reflections.

Sometimes dark clouds form and it looks as if it is starting to rain. But the hot air dries up the rain before it reaches the ground.

24

The Desert's past

In some deserts there are strange tree trunks made of stone. They are fossils of trees that grew in forests there 100 million years ago.

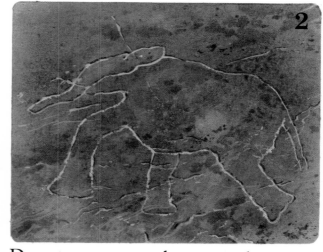

Deserts were not always as dry as they are now. Cave paintings in the Sahara show that animals, such as elephants, once roamed there.

In some places there are ruins of old cities. There was once an oasis here, but the water dried up and the people had to move away.

This plain was once a lake. As the water began to dry up, it got saltier. Then it dried up completely and left a desert covered with salt.

Crossing the Sahara

Geoffrey Moorhouse set out to cross the Sahara in November, 1972, a journey of 5,700 kms.

With an Arab guide, he started from the west coast. They stopped at wells along the way.

He bought new camels at Tidjikja. He wanted to get across the desert before the summer.

They sometimes stayed with nomads they met, who always gave them shelter for the night.

There were few roads or tracks to follow. Moorhouse used a compass to find the way.

Moorhouse was not used to the heat and lack of water. He was very ill but reached Timbuktu.

He rested in the town for six days. Then he hired a new guide and set off again.

They got lost and ran out of water. When they found some, Moorhouse drank 23 pints.

In Mali, Moorhouse was arrested by soldiers. After questions, he was allowed to go on.

Moorhouse hired a new guide, a Tuareg, to take him across the Ahaggar Mountains.

It was almost summer so they walked at night when it was cooler. The camels were dying.

Moorhouse, too ill to go on, stopped in Algeria. He had travelled 3,200 kms in three months.

Making things grow in the Desert

Parts of deserts are becoming even barer because people chop down trees for firewood, or let their herds eat all the plants.

In places steady winds from one direction blow sand towards oases and dunes build up, burying the houses and trees.

Now people are trying to grow crops in the desert. In Iran they spray oil on to sand dunes. This dries to a kind of thick crust.

Trees are planted in it and are protected from animals. When they grow, they help to keep the sand in place and make the soil richer.

Rivers flowing through deserts are dammed, so that water can be channelled to nearby land and used to grow fruit and vegetables.

In Israel plants are grown in plastic tents. When the plants are watered, the plastic stops the water from drying up in the hot sun.

The Imperial Valley in California used to be part of a big desert. Now fruit and vegetables are grown there all the year round.

To make the valley green, a canal was built to bring water from the Colorado river, 128 kilometres away. It is piped to all the fields.

Where the Deserts are

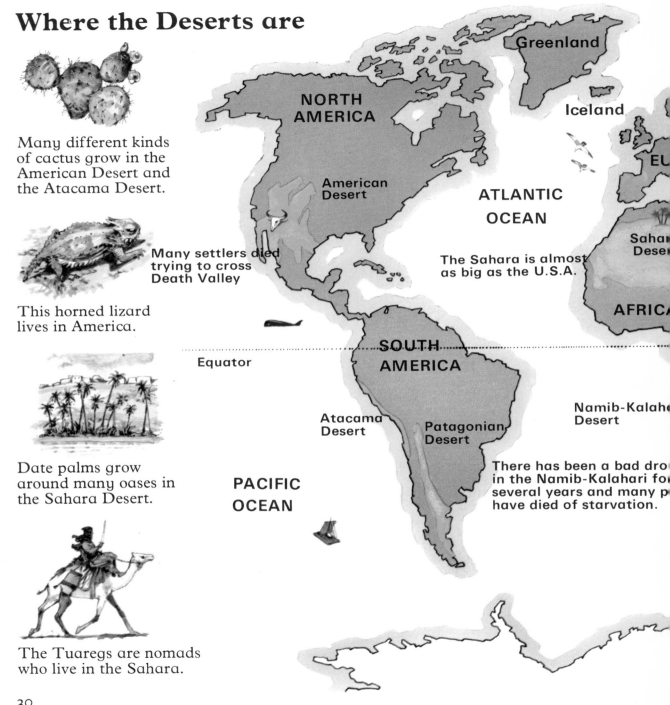

Many different kinds of cactus grow in the American Desert and the Atacama Desert.

This horned lizard lives in America.

Date palms grow around many oases in the Sahara Desert.

The Tuaregs are nomads who live in the Sahara.

Greenland

NORTH AMERICA

Iceland

American Desert

ATLANTIC OCEAN

EU

Sahar Dese

AFRICA

Many settlers died trying to cross Death Valley

The Sahara is almost as big as the U.S.A.

Equator

SOUTH AMERICA

Atacama Desert

Patagonian Desert

Namib-Kalah Desert

PACIFIC OCEAN

There has been a bad dro in the Namib-Kalahari fo several years and many p have died of starvation.

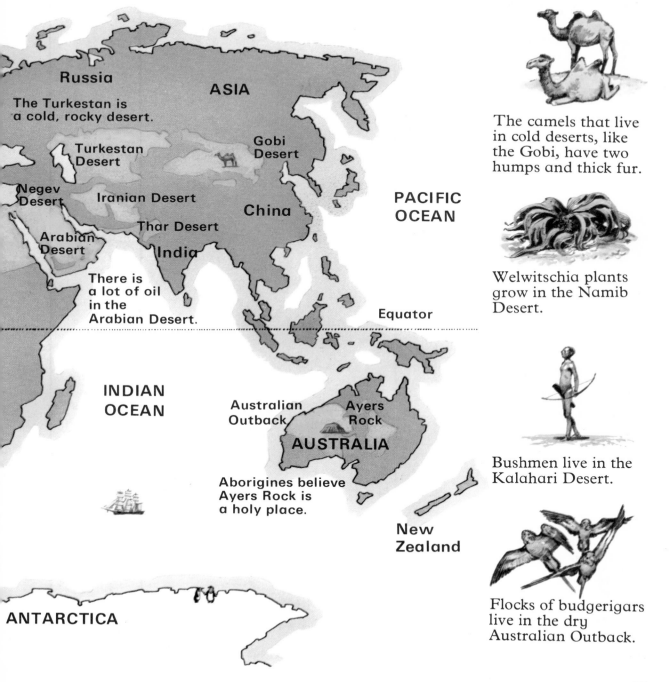

Russia

ASIA

The Turkestan is
a cold, rocky desert.

Turkestan
Desert

Gobi
Desert

Negev
Desert

Iranian Desert

China

PACIFIC
OCEAN

Arabian
Desert

Thar Desert

India

There is
a lot of oil
in the
Arabian Desert.

Equator

INDIAN
OCEAN

Australian
Outback

Ayers
Rock

AUSTRALIA

Aborigines believe
Ayers Rock is
a holy place.

New
Zealand

ANTARCTICA

The camels that live
in cold deserts, like
the Gobi, have two
humps and thick fur.

Welwitschia plants
grow in the Namib
Desert.

Bushmen live in the
Kalahari Desert.

Flocks of budgerigars
live in the dry
Australian Outback.

Facts about Deserts

The biggest desert in the world is the Sahara. It covers an area of 8,400,000 square kilometres, which is nearly a third of Africa.

The world's driest desert is the Atacama Desert on the coast of Chile. Up until 1971, there had been no rain there for nearly 400 years.

Most of the hottest places in the world are in deserts. The hottest countries are in the eastern Sahara.

Deserts are not always hot. The Gobi has cold, snowy winters with temperatures as low as −40 degrees C.

The highest measured sand dune is in Algeria in the northern Sahara. It is 5 kilometres long and 430 metres high.

The shore around the Dead Sea, a lake in the Negev Desert, is the lowest place in the world. It is 393 metres below sea level.

Saguaros are the biggest cacti in the American and Mexican Deserts. They may live to be 200 years old and grow to be 16 metres tall.

© Usborne Publishing Ltd 1980
First published in 1980 by
Usborne Publishing Ltd
20 Garrick Street
London WC2 9BJ, England

The name Usborne and the device are Trade Marks of Usborne Publishing Ltd.

Published in the U.S.A. in 1981 by Hayes Books, 4235 South Memorial Drive, Tulsa, Oklahoma, U.S.A.

Published in Canada by Hayes Publishing Ltd Burlington, Ontario

Printed in Belgium by Casterman, s.a.